Instant Apache Camel Message Routing

Route, transform, split, multicast messages, and do much more with Camel

Bilgin Ibryam

BIRMINGHAM - MUMBAI

Instant Apache Camel Message Routing

First published: August 2013

Production Reference: 1260813

Published by Packt Publishing Ltd.
Livery Place
35 Livery Street
Birmingham B3 2PB, UK.

ISBN 978-1-78328-347-7

www.packtpub.com

Credits

Author
Bilgin Ibryam

Reviewer
Carsten Ringe

Acquisition Editor
Akram Hussain

Commissioning Editor
Priyanka Shah

Technical Editors
Pratik More
Harshad Vairat

Project Coordinator
Michelle Quadros

Proofreader
Linda Morris

Graphics
Ronak Dhruv
Yuvraj Mannari

Production Coordinator
Kirtee Shingan

Cover Work
Kirtee Shingan

Cover Image
Sheetal Aute

About the Author

Bilgin Ibryam is a software engineer with Master's degree in Computer Science and currently working for BBC in London. He is interested in a variety of technologies including application integration, message-oriented middleware, service-oriented architecture, and ERP systems. He is also an open source enthusiast, Apache OFBiz, and Apache Camel committer. In his spare time, he enjoys contributing to open source projects and blogging at www.ofbizian.com.

Bilgin can be contacted via Twitter at https://twitter.com/bibryam.

About the Reviewer

Carsten Ringe has been in the IT industry for almost 10 years now. After studying Electrotechnical Engineering at the University of Applied Sciences in Ostwestfalen-Lippe, he decided to follow his passion and focus his career on software development. Since then, he has been working in the following industries: Automation, Defense, Agriculture, and Logistics. He has experience in utilizing Web technologies such as Websphere, Jboss, and is striving for continuous deployments in his projects whenever possible. His current projects are based on Jboss ESB and Camel, and focus on the integration of logistic partners.

www.PacktPub.com

Support files, eBooks, discount offers and more

You might want to visit www.PacktPub.com for support files and downloads related to your book.

Did you know that Packt offers eBook versions of every book published, with PDF and ePub files available? You can upgrade to the eBook version at www.PacktPub.com and as a print book customer, you are entitled to a discount on the eBook copy. Get in touch with us at service@packtpub.com for more details.

At www.PacktPub.com, you can also read a collection of free technical articles, sign up for a range of free newsletters and receive exclusive discounts and offers on Packt books and eBooks.

http://PacktLib.PacktPub.com

Do you need instant solutions to your IT questions? PacktLib is Packt's online digital book library. Here, you can access, read and search across Packt's entire library of books.

Why Subscribe?

- ▶ Fully searchable across every book published by Packt
- ▶ Copy and paste, print and bookmark content
- ▶ On demand and accessible via web browser

Free Access for Packt account holders

If you have an account with Packt at www.PacktPub.com, you can use this to access PacktLib today and view nine entirely free books. Simply use your login credentials for immediate access.

Table of Contents

Preface   1

Instant Apache Camel Message Routing   5

  Creating a Camel project (Simple)   5

  Routing messages to different destinations (Simple)   10

  Using components (Simple)   14

  Connecting routes (Simple)   17

  Removing unwanted messages (Simple)   21

  Transforming messages (Intermediate)   24

  Splitting a message into many (Intermediate)   28

  Aggregating multiple messages into one (Intermediate)   30

  Reorganizing messages (Intermediate)   34

  Multicasting messages (Intermediate)   36

  Error handling and monitoring (Advanced)   39

  Testing the messaging applications (Advanced)   45

Preface

The world is becoming more connected than ever. There are hundreds of APIs on the Cloud, and more are added every day. Integrating existing systems, creating new applications, which can communicate easily with other applications, is becoming part of the everyday job of developers. Mastering an integration framework like Apache Camel, that can connect to a variety of systems and do message orchestration using well-known Enterprise Integration Patterns, is essential for any software engineer.

What this book covers

Creating a Camel project (Simple) provides a high-level overview of Camel architecture, and demonstrates how to create a simple message driven application.

Routing messages to different destinations (Simple) explains the message structure in Camel, and how to use it for routing messages with a Content-Based Router pattern.

Using components (Simple) shows how Camel utilizes URLs to configure components, and connect to a variety of systems.

Connecting routes (Simple) covers Message Exchange Patterns in Camel, and connecting routes with other parts of the applications.

Removing unwanted messages (Simple) introduces Message Filter and Idempotent Consumer patterns along with the powerful Bean Binding feature.

Transforming messages (Intermediate) demonstrates a variety of ways in which message transformations happens in Camel applications.

Splitting a message into many (Intermediate) presents the Splitter pattern and how the Camel threading model works.

Aggregating multiple messages into one (Intermediate) shows the Aggregator pattern and its usage in other patterns, such as Scatter-Gather and Composed Message Processor.

Reorganizing messages (Intermediate) introduces three more patterns used for changing the message order and frequency: Resequencer, Throttler, and Delayer.

Multicasting messages (Intermediate) shows how to send a message to multiple recipients using Recipient List and Wire Tap patterns.

Error handling and monitoring (Advanced) explains the Dead Letter Channel pattern, and the different techniques used in Camel for monitoring and dealing with errors.

Testing the messaging applications (Advanced) presents the different tools provided by Camel for testing the routing logic.

What you need for this book

In order to run the examples accompanying this book, you will need Java 6 or higher, Apache Maven 2.2.1 or higher, and Apache Camel version 2.11 or higher.

Who this book is for

This book is intended for Java developers who are new to Apache Camel and message oriented applications. It shows how to do application integration using the industry standard Enterprise Integration Patterns.

Conventions

In this book, you will find a number of styles of text that distinguish between different kinds of information. Here are some examples of these styles, and an explanation of their meaning.

Code words in text, database table names, folder names, filenames, file extensions, pathnames, dummy URLs, user input, and Twitter handles are shown as follows: "In the Java DSL, we create a route by extending `RouteBuilder` and overriding the `configure` method."

A block of code is set as follows:

```
<dependency>
    <groupId>org.apache.camel</groupId>
    <artifactId>camel-core</artifactId>
    <version>${camel-version}</version>
</dependency>
```

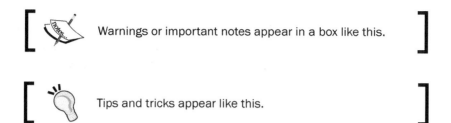

Warnings or important notes appear in a box like this.

Tips and tricks appear like this.

Reader feedback

Feedback from our readers is always welcome. Let us know what you think about this book—what you liked or may have disliked. Reader feedback is important for us to develop titles that you really get the most out of.

To send us general feedback, simply send an e-mail to feedback@packtpub.com, and mention the book title via the subject of your message.

If there is a topic that you have expertise in and you are interested in either writing or contributing to a book, see our author guide on www.packtpub.com/authors.

Customer support

Now that you are the proud owner of a Packt book, we have a number of things to help you to get the most from your purchase.

Downloading the example code

You can download the example code files for all Packt books you have purchased from your account at http://www.packtpub.com. If you purchased this book elsewhere, you can visit http://www.packtpub.com/support and register to have the files e-mailed directly to you. You can also download the example code files for this book from github at https://github.com/bibryam/camel-message-routing-examples.

Errata

Although we have taken every care to ensure the accuracy of our content, mistakes do happen. If you find a mistake in one of our books—maybe a mistake in the text or the code—we would be grateful if you would report this to us. By doing so, you can save other readers from frustration and help us improve subsequent versions of this book. If you find any errata, please report them by visiting http://www.packtpub.com/submit-errata, selecting your book, clicking on the **errata submission form** link, and entering the details of your errata. Once your errata are verified, your submission will be accepted and the errata will be uploaded on our website, or added to any list of existing errata, under the Errata section of that title. Any existing errata can be viewed by selecting your title from http://www.packtpub.com/support.

Piracy

Piracy of copyright material on the Internet is an ongoing problem across all media. At Packt, we take the protection of our copyright and licenses very seriously. If you come across any illegal copies of our works, in any form, on the Internet, please provide us with the location address or website name immediately so that we can pursue a remedy.

Please contact us at copyright@packtpub.com with a link to the suspected pirated material.

We appreciate your help in protecting our authors, and our ability to bring you valuable content.

Questions

You can contact us at questions@packtpub.com if you are having a problem with any aspect of the book, and we will do our best to address it.

Instant Apache Camel Message Routing

Apache Camel is the most popular open source integration framework, which continues growing at a fast pace, thanks to its active community and ease of use. *Instant Apache Camel Message Routing* is a quick introduction to application integration using Apache Camel. It shows how to create messaging applications leveraging the industry standard Enterprise Integration Patterns (EIP).

Creating a Camel project (Simple)

Camel is a Java based application integration framework. It is lightweight and can run as a standalone application, as part of spring applications, or as an OSGI bundle. Camel can easily connect with many different systems using a variety of connectors, and integrate seamlessly, thanks to multiple messaging pattern implementations. In this first Camel application, we are going to connect to the filesystem and copy files from the source folder to a target folder using a polling consumer.

Getting ready

For the examples in this book, we are going to use Apache Camel version 2.11 (http://camel.apache.org/) and Apache Maven version 2.2.1 or newer (http://maven.apache.org/) as a build tool. Both of these projects can be downloaded for free from their websites. The complete source code for all the examples in this book is available on github at https://github.com/bibryam/camel-message-routing-examples repository. It contains Camel routes in Spring XML and Java DSL with accompanying unit tests. The source code for this tutorial is located under the project: camel-message-routing-examples/creating-camel-project.

How to do it...

1. In a new Maven project add the following Camel dependency to the `pom.xml`:

```xml
<dependency>
    <groupId>org.apache.camel</groupId>
    <artifactId>camel-core</artifactId>
    <version>${camel-version}</version>
</dependency>
```

2. With this dependency in place, creating our first route requires only a couple of lines of Java code:

```java
public class MoveFileRoute extends RouteBuilder {
    @Override
    public void configure() throws Exception {
        from("file://source")
            .to("log://org.apache.camel.howto?showAll=true")
            .to("file://target");
    }
}
```

3. Once the route is defined, the next step is to add it to CamelContext, which is the actual routing engine and run it as a standalone Java application:

```java
public class Main {
    public static void main(String[] args) throws Exception
    {
        CamelContext camelContext = new
    DefaultCamelContext();
        camelContext.addRoutes(new MoveFileRoute());
        camelContext.start();
        Thread.sleep(10000);
        camelContext.stop();
    }
}
```

That's all it takes to create our first Camel application. Now, we can run it using a Java IDE or from the command line with Maven `mvn exec:java`.

Downloading the example code

You can download the example code files for all Packt books you have purchased from your account at http://www.packtpub.com. If you purchased this book elsewhere, you can visit http://www.packtpub.com/support and register to have the files e-mailed directly to you.

How it works...

Camel has a modular architecture; its core (camel-core dependency) contains all the functionality needed to run a Camel application—DSL for various languages, the routing engine, implementations of EIPs, a number of data converters, and core components. This is the only dependency needed to run this application. Then there are optional technology specific connector dependencies (called components) such as JMS, SOAP, JDBC, Twitter, and so on, which are not needed for this example, as the file and log components we used are all part of the camel-core.

Camel routes are created using a **Domain Specific Language** (**DSL**), specifically tailored for application integration. Camel DSLs are high-level languages that allow us to easily create routes, combining various processing steps and EIPs without going into low-level implementation details. In the Java DSL, we create a route by extending `RouteBuilder` and overriding the `configure` method. A route represents a chain of processing steps applied to a message based on some rules. The route has a beginning defined by the `from` endpoint, and one or more processing steps commonly called "Processors" (which implement the `Processor` interface).

 Most of these ideas and concepts originate from the Pipes and Filters pattern from the *Enterprise Integration Patterns* book by Gregor Hohpe and Bobby Woolf. The book provides an extensive list of patterns, which are also available at `http://www.enterpriseintegrationpatterns.com`, and the majority of which are implemented by Camel.

With the Pipes and Filters pattern, a large processing task is divided into a sequence of smaller independent processing steps (Filters) that are connected by channels (Pipes). Each filter processes messages received from the inbound channel, and publishes the result to the outbound channel. In our route, the processing steps are reading the file using a polling consumer, logging it and writing the file to the target folder, all of them piped by Camel in the sequence specified in the DSL. We can visualize the individual steps in the application with the following diagram:

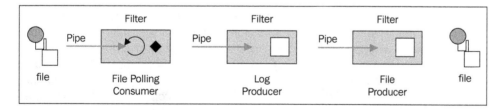

A route has exactly one input called consumer and identified by the keyword `from`. A consumer receives messages from producers or external systems, wraps them in a Camel specific format called `Exchange`, and starts routing them. There are two types of consumers: a polling consumer that fetches messages periodically (for example, reading files from a folder) and an event-driven consumer that listens for events and gets activated when a message arrives (for example, an HTTP server). All the other processor nodes in the route are either a type of integration pattern or producers used for sending messages to various endpoints. Producers are identified by the keyword to and they are capable of converting exchanges and delivering them to other channels using the underlying transport mechanism. In our example, the log producer logs the files using the `log4J API`, whereas the file producer writes them to a target folder.

The route is not enough to have a running application; it is only a template that defines the processing steps. The engine that runs and manages the routes is called **Camel Context**. A high level view of `CamelContext` looks like the following diagram:

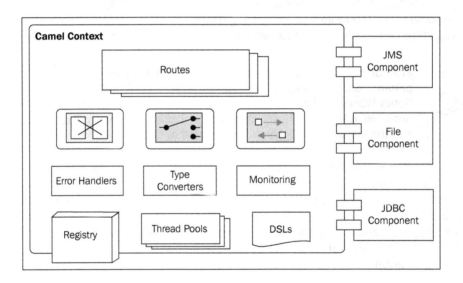

`CamelContext` is a dynamic multithread route container, responsible for managing all aspects of the routing: route lifecycle, message conversions, configurations, error handling, monitoring, and so on. When `CamelContext` is started, it starts the components, endpoints and activates the routes. The routes are kept running until `CamelContext` is stopped again when it performs a graceful shutdown giving time for all the in-flight messages to complete processing. `CamelContext` is dynamic, it allows us to start, stop routes, add new routes, or remove running routes at runtime. In our example, after adding the `MoveFileRoute`, we start `CamelContext` and let it copy files for 10 seconds, and then the application terminates. If we check the target folder, we should see files copied from the source folder.

There's more...

Camel applications can run as standalone applications or can be embedded in other containers such as Spring or Apache Karaf. To make development and deployment to various environments easy, Camel provides a number of DSLs, including Spring XML, Blueprint XML, Groovy, and Scala. Next, we will have a look at the Spring XML DSL.

Using Spring XML DSL

Java and Spring XML are the two most popular DSLs in Camel. Both provide access to all Camel features and the choice is mostly a matter of taste. Java DSL is more flexible and requires fewer lines of code, but can easily become complicated and harder to understand with the use of anonymous inner classes and other Java constructs. Spring XML DSL, on the other hand, is easier to read and maintain, but it is too verbose and testing it requires a little more effort. My rule of thumb is to use Spring XML DSL only when Camel is going to be part of a Spring application (to benefit from other Spring features available in Camel), or when the routing logic has to be easily understood by many people.

For the routing examples in the book, we are going to show a mixture of Java and Spring XML DSL, but the source code accompanying this book has all the examples in both DSLs. In order to use Spring, we also need the following dependency in our projects:

```
<dependency>
    <groupId>org.apache.camel</groupId>
    <artifactId>camel-spring</artifactId>
    <version>${camel-version}</version>
</dependency>
```

The same application for copying files, written in Spring XML DSL looks like the following:

```
<beans xmlns="http://www.springframework.org/schema/beans"
        xmlns:xsi="http://www.w3.org/2001/XMLSchema-instance"
        xsi:schemaLocation="
        http://www.springframework.org/schema/beans
   http://www.springframework.org/schema/beans/spring-beans.xsd
        http://camel.apache.org/schema/spring
   http://camel.apache.org/schema/spring/camel-spring.xsd">
<camelContext xmlns="http://camel.apache.org/schema/spring">
    <route>
        <from uri="file://source"/>
            <to uri="log://org.apache.camel.howto?showAll=true"/>
            <to uri="file://target"/>
    </route>
</camelContext>
</beans>
```

Notice that this is a standard Spring XML file with an additional `CamelContext` element containing the route. We can launch the Spring application as part of a web application, OSGI bundle, or as a standalone application:

```
public static void main(String[] args) throws Exception {
    AbstractApplicationContext springContext = new ClassPathXmlApplica
tionContext("META-INF/spring/move-file-context.xml");
    springContext.start();
    Thread.sleep(10000);
    springContext.stop();
}
```

When the Spring container starts, it will instantiate a `CamelContext`, start it and add the routes without any other code required. That is the complete application written in Spring XML DSL. More information about Spring support in Apache Camel can be found at `http://camel.apache.org/spring.html`.

Routing messages to different destinations (Simple)

In the previous tutorial, we routed all the messages through the same processing steps. Integrating real applications usually involves more complex routing scenarios where each message type is processed differently. In this tutorial, we are going to route a message into different locations based on the message content, using a Context-Based Router pattern.

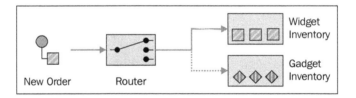

Getting ready

The complete source code for this tutorial is located under the following project: `camel-message-routing-examples/routing-different-destinations`.

How to do it...

We will extend the previous example by adding conditions to direct incoming files into different folders based on file names:

```
from("file://source")
      .choice()
```

```
        .when(simple("${in.header.CamelFileName} contains
'widget.txt'"))
            .to("file://widget")
        .when(simple("${in.header.CamelFileName} contains
'gadget.txt'"))
            .to("file://gadget")
        .otherwise()
            .to("log://org.apache.camel.howto?showAll=true");
```

How it works...

A Context-Based Router is similar to a `switch` statement or to the `if then-elseif` statement in Java. The incoming message will be directed to one of the possible channels, depending on the condition that is evaluated, usually against the message content. In our example, there are three possible destinations for the incoming messages, and the conditions are written using Simple language. The condition has to be a predicate, that is, an expression that returns only true or false. If the result is true, the message is routed into that channel of the Context-Based Router, otherwise the next condition in order is evaluated. Similar to the `default` case in a Java `switch` statement, there is an optional `otherwise` element for this pattern. If the message doesn't match any of the predicates, it will be directed to the default channel of the route.

Camel expressions operate on the routed message and are used as part of various integration patterns. There are two types of expressions: one that implements the **Expression** interface and can produce a value from any type, and the other that implements the **Predicate** interface and produces a Boolean result. Expressions give access to all parts of the routed message, which in Camel world is represented by the `Exchange` class and has the following structure:

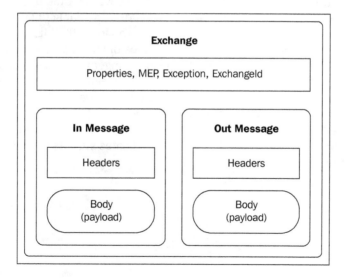

The `Exchange` class wraps the mandatory `In Message` representing the request data coming from an inbound channel, and an optional `Out Message` for the response going into an outbound channel. Each message consists of a payload called `Body` with Object type and `Headers`, which is a Map for storing key-value pairs associated with the message. The `Exchange` class also has `Properties` for storing Camel specific data, `Message Exchange Pattern` (MEP), `ExchangeId`, and `Exception` field for tracking exceptions if any were encountered during routing. Usually, when a processor receives `Exchange`, it reads the data from `In Message` (including `Body` and `Headers`), and depending on MEP writes the processed results to `Out Message` or updates `In Message`, to be passed to the next processor in the route. In our example, file consumer reads a file from the source folder then puts its reference to the message body, and populates various headers with information about the file (this is where the `CamelFileName` header gets populated). Then the expressions in the Context-Based Router retrieve the file name from the headers and do the comparison. If the file name contains the string `widget.txt` the message is sent to the `widget` folder, otherwise the next condition is evaluated which does a similar comparison with the `gadget.txt` string. If the message doesn't satisfy any of the conditions, it is sent to the default channel where it is logged and not written to any folder.

There's more...

Next, we will have a look at the other expression languages that Camel supports, and how to make the routing even more dynamic, using Java beans for deciding which is the next endpoint for a message.

Expression languages

The `Predicate` statement used in the previous example was created using Simple language, but there are many other supported languages. It includes popular scripting languages such as Beanshell, Groovy, Ruby, Python and languages for working with XML, such as XPath, XQuery, the Unified EL, OGNL, among others. The choice of language usually depends on the message format and personal preferences, but Simple language is flexible enough for most occasions. Simple language is a home grown language developed by the Camel community for writing powerful expressions. It gives easy access to different parts of the `Exchange`, such as input body `${in.body}` or a specific message header `${in.header.userId}`, properties `{property.someKey}`, environment variables `${sysenv.someOtherKet}`, and so on. It also has good operator support used mostly for predicates such as `>=`, `contains`, `!=`, `regex`, `&&`, `||`, and so on.

Dynamic routing

A Context-Based Router can direct a message to the correct recipient if all the recipients are known in advance. All of the outbound channels of the Context-Based Router have to be specified as part of its definition, and only then it can choose one based on the message content. This introduces a dependency of the router to all possible destinations and prevents it from choosing a destination dynamically. Dynamic Router pattern solves this problem by choosing a destination for each message at runtime, and configuring itself using control messages from each participating destination.

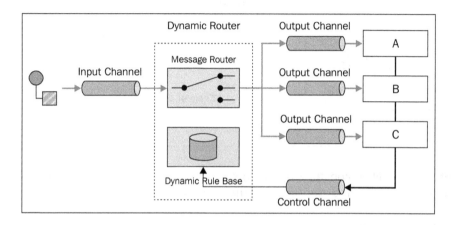

In Camel, a Dynamic Router pattern is implemented with the `dynamicRouter` statement that accepts an expression to determine where the message should go next. After routing the message, the expression is evaluated again using the updated message to determine where the message should be routed next. Evaluating the expression and routing the message continues until the expression returns null to indicate the end of routing for that message. So it is important for the expression to return null at some point, otherwise Camel will continue routing the same message endlessly. Because of this complex nature, `dynamicRouter` expressions usually use Bean expressions:

```
from("direct:start")
    .dynamicRouter(method(DestinationChooser.class,
      "nextEndpoint"));
```

 For an example using the Dynamic Router, have a look at
http://camel.apache.org/dynamic-router.html.

Using components (Simple)

As of this writing Camel has around 150 components with support for many protocols and technologies. The full list of components is available at `http://camel.apache.org/components.html` with links to each component's details page where all the configuration options are explained. A component represents an adapter for a specific API and allows Camel to exchange messages with external applications. The following diagram depicts how components enable external applications sending data to a messaging channel using components' endpoints and also receive data from it:

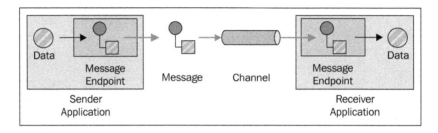

In this tutorial, we will demonstrate how to leverage Camel components by creating an HTTP endpoint, and calling external services with the Jetty component.

Getting ready

The complete source code for this tutorial is located under the project `camel-message-routing-examples/using-components`.

How to do it...

Camel-core contains a dozen components which are always available with Camel. These include `bean`, `direct`, `vm`, `file`, `log`, `mock`, `seda`, `timer`, `xslt`, and a few more. All of the other components used for routing have to be retrieved and added additionally to the classpath.

1. In this tutorial, we will use the jetty component, so the following camel-jetty dependency will be needed:

```
<dependency>
    <groupId>org.apache.camel</groupId>
    <artifactId>camel-jetty</artifactId>
    <version>${camel-version}</version>
</dependency>
```

2. Next, we will create a route with Jetty consumer and log the messages using log component. Finally, we use a Jetty producer to make external HTTP calls to Google.

```
from("jetty:http://localhost:8181?matchOnUriPrefix=true")
    .to("log://org.apache.camel.howto?showAll=true")
  .to("jetty:http://www.google.co.uk?bridgeEndpoint=true&throwExcept
    ionOnFailure=false");
```

When this route is started, it will start a Jetty web server listening on localhost port 8080. If we use a web browser and try to access http://localhost:8080, the route will log the request, make an HTTP call to http://www.google.co.uk, and return the result to the requestor. And, what we should see in our browser (if all works fine) is Google's home page. So this route is in fact an HTTP proxy that logs all requests.

How it works...

Routes in Camel consist of EIPs and components. EIPs transform the messages inside the routes, whereas components usually allow messages to reach external systems. Components can be added to Camel runtime (CamelContext) in two ways. The less popular way is manually instantiating a component and adding it to the context:

```
camelContext.addComponent("jetty", new JettyHttpComponent());
```

The second way of adding components to Camel runtime is through the auto-discovery mechanism. In this mode, when a component is needed as part of the routing process and it is not available to CamelContext, Camel will scan the classpath and look at META-INF/services/org/apache/camel/component for a file matching the component name. The jetty component's file META-INF/services/org/apache/camel/component/jetty contains the following:

```
class=org.apache.camel.component.jetty.JettyHttpComponent
```

The content of the file shows the actual component class, so that Camel can instantiate it, and add it to CamelContext. A component is in essence an endpoint factory, it creates endpoints based on URLs. The Endpoint interface models the end of channel through which systems can send and receive messages. Camel endpoints are usually referenced using URLs. URLs provide a unified way for describing endpoints for various systems. The Camel URL has the following structure: schema:context path:options. For example, the Jetty URL from the previous route looks like:

```
jetty://http://www.google.co.uk?bridgeEndpoint=true&throwExceptionOnF
ailure=false
```

Its schema is jetty, which tells Camel what is the component class name, that the context path is `http://www.google.co.uk` and it has two options `bridgeEndpoint=true&thr owExceptionOnFailure=false`. The context path is endpoint specific; it means different things for different endpoints. For example, the context path of the log endpoint used above `org.apache.camel.howto` represents the logging category, whereas in Jetty it is the host and port name. Options are also endpoint specific, and each endpoint has different options for the underlying technology. Once an endpoint is instantiated for a specific URL, then it is responsible for creating consumers and producers.

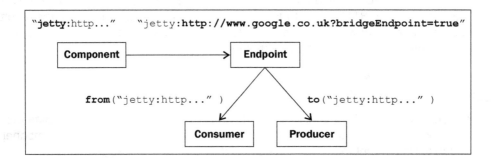

At a very high level, the process of using a component in a Camel route goes through the following steps: when a URI is used in a route, based on the URI schema, a component is instantiated. The component uses the context path and the options to create an endpoint. Then the endpoint creates a consumer or producer depending on what is needed in the route. When the consumer receives a message from the external system, it transforms the message to an exchange and starts routing it in Camel. The producer, on the other hand, receives an exchange as part of the routing, and delivers it to the external system using the external API.

There's more...

We saw how to pass primitive types and string literals as `Endpoint` options. Next, we will see how Camel offers a unified access to the environment it is running on, and how to pass complex objects from its environment as options in the URLs.

Accessing the Registry

Camel **Registry** provides a unified interface for accessing Java beans on the runtime environment. There are different `Registry` implementations and depending on our DSL choice, one is always in use. If we use the Java DSL, by default the `Registry` will be `JndiRegistry`. This `Registry` uses Java Naming and Directory Interface (JNDI) to lookup beans. There is also a simpler Map based `Registry` available to use with Java DSL. With `SimpleRegistry`, we can manually add bean instances to make them available during routing:

```
SimpleRegistry registry = new SimpleRegistry();
registry.put("myHttpClient", new HttpClient());
CamelContext context = new DefaultCamelContext(registry);
```

Once a bean is available in the `Registry`, we can pass it as an option to an endpoint by prefixing its key with #. For example, the Jetty producer has an option called `httpClient` for setting a custom `HttpClient`, and we can pass our instance from the `SimpleRegistry`, as shown in the following code:

```
.to("jetty:http://www.google.co.uk?bridgeEndpoint=true&httpClient=
    #myHttpClient");
```

Options are usually fields on the concrete `Endpoint` implementation, and to set the `httpClient` field of `JettyHttpEndpoint`, Camel will look up the `Registry` using `myHttpClient` as the key.

When Spring XML DSL is used, the `Registry` implementation is provided by the `ApplicationContextRegistry` class, which gives access to the beans from the Spring `ApplicationContext`. So, if we have a Spring bean declaration like the following line of code, we can access it as `Endpoint` options with the same syntax as the previous `#myHttpClient`:

```
<bean id="myHttpClient"
  class="org.eclipse.jetty.client.HttpClient"/>
```

There is also an `OsgiServiceRegistry` implementation used when running Camel in the OSGI container and giving access to the beans from the OSGI service registry.

Connecting routes (Simple)

A Camel route is the minimum self contained unit of messaging logic. It has a beginning, one or many processing steps, an end, its own lifecycle, error handlers, and so on. Any integration application of a reasonable size consists of multiple routes working simultaneously to achieve a common goal. In many terms, routes are similar to objects in the object oriented world. Routes have responsibilities and also interact with their peers, hosted on the same `CamelContext` or even a separate `CamelContext` in the same JVM. In this tutorial, we are going to see how to connect routes with one another and other Java codes.

Getting ready

The complete source code for this tutorial is located under the project, `camel-message-routing-examples/connecting-routes`.

How to do it...

1. Create a route using the timer component to generate a message per second. Add a processor to log the messages, and then send them to the next route created as follows:

    ```
    <route>
        <from uri="timer://start?fixedRate=true&amp;period=1000"/>
        <to uri="log://org.apache.camel.generator?level=INFO"/>
        <to uri="direct:logger"/>
    </route>
    ```

2. Then, let's create a route that receives messages from the previous route using the direct consumer and logs them.

    ```
    <route>
        <from uri="direct:logger"/>
        <to uri="log://org.apache.camel.logger?level=INFO"/>
        <to uri="mock:result"/>
    </route>
    ```

How it works...

Typical reasons for splitting a routing logic into multiple smaller routes are transaction boundaries, different error handling strategies for different parts of the application, code reuse, testability, and so on. In our example, we created two routes only to demonstrate the direct component usage. Direct component, as the name suggests, provides direct synchronous invocation of the consumer when a message is sent to that endpoint using a direct producer. Each direct endpoint is identified by a unique name in `CamelContext`, and it can have only one consumer that receives messages and one or multiple producers. In our example, route one sends messages to `direct:logger` using a direct producer, and route two consumes from the same endpoint.

Using direct component allows connecting two routes as if they were one route: the message flows through all processors of the first route, then the second one and returns control back to the consumer of the first route for the next message. Because it is synchronous invocation (literally direct producer invokes the direct consumer method) and uses the same thread for processing the messages in both routes, it is also possible to make both routes participate in the same transaction when a transacted route is created.

Another thing to notice is that we started using mock component. Mock endpoints collect all the exchanges they receive and allow us write tests and verify the routing logic. In a real word application, instead of having mock endpoints hardcoded in the route we would have other endpoints for further processing the messages and replace them with mock endpoints during testing. We can see how mock endpoints are used by looking at the unit tests accompanying each route, and we will also demonstrate how to use them in the later part of this book.

There's more...

In addition to synchronous route connections, Camel also lets us connect routes asynchronously, connect routes which are in different `CamelContexts`, and also exchange messages with routes from custom Java code.

Asynchronous connection

Another option for connecting routes is to use the SEDA (Staged Event Driven Architecture) component. SEDA provides asynchronous behavior, where messages are exchanged using an inmemory `BlockingQueue`. When this component is used, the producer sends a message and instantly returns to process the next message while letting the second route to process the messages using its own thread pool. This decoupling of routing threads allows us to implement patterns such as Competing Consumers (by setting the `concurrentConsumers` option to a number greater than 1) or a Publish-Subscribe pattern (by setting the `multipleConsumers` option to `true`). With the Competing Consumers pattern, a message is delivered to only one from multiple consumers, allowing concurrent processing, whereas with Publish-Subscribe patterns each consumer receives a copy of the published messages. This component is ideal for situations when there is a long running task, and to prevent from blocking the whole route, we could create a separate route for the long running task and connect it to the main route using a SEDA component. With this approach, long running tasks will be processed by a separate thread on the subroute keeping the main route unblocked.

One important concept in Camel, which is also related to the SEDA component, is the message exchange pattern. Camel messages are either one way event messages (InOnly) or request reply (InOut). By default, many components use an InOnly exchange pattern, but we can specify the exchange pattern explicitly as part of the endpoint invocation:

```
from("activemq:someQueue")
    .inOnly("seda:nextRoute");
```

We can also specify it as a part of the route:

```
from("mq:someQueue")
    .setExchangePattern(ExchangePattern.InOut)
    .to("mock:result");
```

With one way messaging (which is also known as fire and forget) the sender doesn't expect a response from the receiver, whereas with request reply style messaging a response is expected. The `Exchange` object keeps track of MEP and handles one way messages with its `In Message` field, and uses `Out Message` when a response is expected.

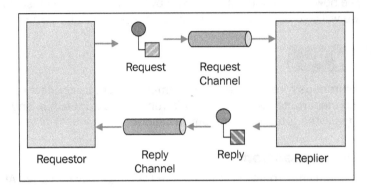

We can see the different ways for explicitly specifying the exchange pattern at `http://camel.apache.org/request-reply.html`.

The SEDA component will behave differently depending on the MEP. If the MEP is InOnly, the SEDA producer puts the message to the queue and continues with the next message without waiting for it to be processed. But, if the MEP is InOut, after passing the message it will block and wait for it to be processed (by a different thread from the SEDA consumer) or timeout occurs. This default behavior can be controlled with the `waitForTaskToComplete` option, where setting it to `Always` will make it always wait for the exchange to be processed and setting a value to `Never` will prevent it from waiting, regardless of the messaging pattern. We can see all the options available to the SEDA component at `http://camel.apache.org/seda.html`.

Connecting routes in the same JVM

Direct and SEDA components connect routes running within the same `CamelContext`. To connect routes running in separate `CamelContexts`, but in the same JVM, there are two other components: vm and direct-vm. The vm component extends SEDA, and direct-vm extends direct to provide communication across the `CamelContext` instances. They can connect, for example, separate Camel application bundles running in the same OSGI container or separate war files running in the same web-container such as Tomcat. Internally these components are implemented using static fields, so it is important that the applications share the same `camel-core.jar` on their classpath. With an OSGI container, this is done by having one version of camel-core used by Camel applications wanting to communicate and with Tomcat it is achieved by placing the `camel-core.jar` file in the `ext` directory as opposed to each WAR file.

Calling routes from Java methods

Routes can send and receive messages among them, but it is also possible to do the same from our Java code. To send a message to a route, create a `ProducerTemplate` (named after Spring templates) from `CamelContext`, and then send messages to the consumer using direct component:

```
ProducerTemplate producerTemplate =
    camelContext.createProducerTemplate();
template.sendBody("direct:logger", "<hello>world!</hello>");
```

Notice that with `producerTemplate` we can send messages directly to any endpoint even if they are not part of a route. For example, the following line of code will send the message directly to an `ActiveMQ` queue without a need for a route:

```
template.sendBody("activemq:my.queue", "<hello>world!</hello>");
```

`ProducerTemplate` has mainly two kinds of methods: `send*` method which performs fire and forget style InOnly messages, and also `request*` method which do request-reply style InOut messages returning the processed result.

In a similar fashion, there is also `ConsumerTemplate` for receiving messages from an endpoint:

```
ConsumerTemplate consumerTemplate =
    camelContext().createConsumerTemplate();
String result = consumerTemplate.receiveBody("activemq:my.queue",
    String.class);
```

The `consumerTemplate` in the previous code snippet will retrieve a message from `ActiveMQ` and return the message body as string.

Removing unwanted messages (Simple)

Not all messages are interesting and worth processing. Some applications generate too much noise, and only messages matching criteria should continue down a pipeline. In these kind of situations Message Filter pattern is used to eliminate undesirable messages, as shown in the following figure:

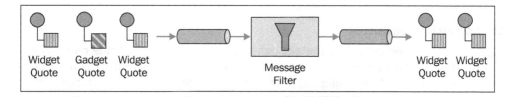

Getting ready

The complete source code for this tutorial is located under the following project:
`camel-message-routing-examples/removing-unwanted-messages`.

How to do it...

Start with a filter definition, followed by a predicate expression and the processors to which this filter applies:

```
from("direct:start")
    .filter(header("userStatus").isEqualTo("valid"))
        .to("mock:valid")
    .end()
    .to("mock:all");
```

In the Java DSL, optionally we can mark the end of the filter, specifying up to where the filter applies. If not specified it applies for the rest of the route.

How it works...

This pattern is a simpler version of the Context-Based Router pattern demonstrated in the previous tutorial. It is conceptually similar to a Java `if` statement. If the incoming message satisfies the condition specified in the filter, the message is passed to the child processors. If the message fails to satisfy the condition, it is discarded and not passed to the child processor. In our example, we let only messages with valid `userStatus` header reach the `mock:valid` endpoint. None of the other messages will be passed to the `mock:valid` endpoint. Note that when a message is filtered out, it is not totally stopped from routing, it is not passed to child processors but it continues routing after the filter element. There is another command called `stop` that is used to completely stop a message from being processed further.

There's more...

Filtering messages is a very common operation in pipelines. Next, we will have a look at a special type of filter, the Idempotent consumer, and how to use Java beans for filtering messages, and as part of routes in general.

Idempotent consumer

One special kind of filter is the **Idempotent consumer** used to filter duplicate messages. The term idempotent describes a function that produces the same result if it is applied to itself. In computing, an idempotent operation has no additional effect when called more than once with the same input parameters. In messaging applications this means that receiving the same message once or multiple times has the same effect. Camel implements this pattern using the `IdempotentConsumer` class which uses an `Expression` to calculate a unique message ID for each message:

```
import static
  org.apache.camel.processor.idempotent.MemoryIdempotentRepository.m
    emoryIdempotentRepository;
from("direct:start")
    .idempotentConsumer(
header("messageId"), memoryIdempotentRepository())
    .to("mock:result");
```

This ID is then looked up in `IdempotentRepository` to see if it has been processed before; if it has the message is discarded; if it hasn't then the message is processed and the ID is added to the repository to prevent processing other messages with the same ID.

Bean binding

When expressions are not flexible enough or we want to reuse existing Java code as part of EIPs, Camel bean language allows us to call Java methods directly from routes. Here is a filter that uses the method expression to call a bean method:

```
filter().method("myFilterBean", "isValidRequest")
```

Camel will look up in the `Registry` for a bean with the ID `myFilterBean` and call its `isValidRequest` method. In this case, because it is a predicate expression used in filter, the method has to return a Boolean or a value convertible to a Boolean. Instead of a reference to a bean, we can specify a class or omit the method name. Camel will instantiate an object from the class and if the method name is missing, it will attempt to choose the best matching method to call using its sophisticated bean binding algorithm. When a message arrives, it will try to map the `Exchange` content to method parameters and convert the result to an appropriate type. Some Camel specific types, such as `Exchange`, `Message`, `Registry`, `CamelContext`, and so on are always provided, if present, as method parameters. Camel will also try to bind the message body as the first parameter of the method by doing any type conversion optionally, unless it is one of the Camel specific types mentioned previously. We can influence the way parameters' values are created from the `Exchange` by using binding annotations in our beam:

```
public boolean isValidRequest(@Header("userId") String userId,
    @Body String body, Exchange exchange)
```

By annotating the method parameters, we tell Camel to bind the `userId` header to the first parameter, the message body to the second, and the Camel specific type, `Exchange`, to the last parameters. If we want to have cleaner POJOs, without any Camel dependencies, we could bind parameters using method options instead of introducing annotations in our beans. With this approach we don't need to touch the POJOs, instead we specify the parameter mappings in the route:

```
filter().method("myFilterBean", "isValidRequest(@Header("userId"),
    ${body}, null)")
```

Notice, with this approach we can additionally use literals (Booleans, numbers, string, null) or Simple language enclosed in curly brackets to pass values to the method.

Method construct is an expression, which can be used as part of EIPs (such as Message Filter, Context-Based Router, and so on), but Camel also has a bean component, which can be used as a processor in the routes using the same bean binding rules:

```
from(...)
    .bean(OrderService.class, "doSomething(${body},
${header.high})")
```

You can also use `to` instead of bean:

```
from(...)
    .to("bean:orderService?method=doSomething(${body.asXml},
${header.high})")
```

In the preceding code snippet, the beans are not used as expressions in EIPs, they are processors in a route which actually can modify the `Exchange` or take some actions on each message. Bean binding is a very powerful Camel feature allowing us to execute Java code from anywhere in the routes. We can find out more about this feature at `http://camel.apache.org/bean-binding.html`.

Transforming messages (Intermediate)

Very often integration applications have to work with existing systems which have a predefined data format that we cannot change. In other situations, after some processing the data has to be converted to a format that can be understood by external systems. Camel offers many different ways for transforming data from one format into another. In this tutorial we are going to convert XML input into JSON using the xmljson component and will have a look at other ways for doing data transformations.

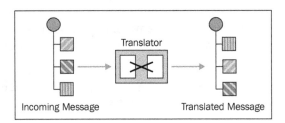

Getting ready

The complete source code for this tutorial is located under the project camel-message-routing-examples/transforming-messages.

In addition to the standard camel-core dependencies, for this tutorial we will need also the xmljson component:

```
<dependency>
    <groupId>org.apache.camel</groupId>
    <artifactId>camel-xmljson</artifactId>
```

```
    <version>${camel-version}</version>
</dependency>
```

How to do it...

1. Within the `dataFormat` element configure an `xmljson` data format and give it an ID.

```
<dataFormats>
    <xmljson id="xmljsonWithOptions" forceTopLevelObject="true"
trimSpaces="true" skipNamespaces="true"
removeNamespacePrefixes="true"/>
</dataFormats>
```

2. Then, add a `marshal` step in the route and reference the `xmljson` data format by its ID.

```
<route>
    <from uri="direct:start"/>
    <marshal ref="xmljsonWithOptions"/>
    <to uri="mock:result"/>
</route>
```

How it works...

Camel data formats are used to transform data between a low-level presentation and a high-level presentation by providing two operations: `marshall` and `unmarshall`. `XmlJson` data format is marshaling from XML to JSON and unmarshaling from a JSON to XML format. There are other data formats that convert from Java to XML and JSON or vice versa, but all of them require a POJO. The difference for this data format is that it doesn't require a POJO for the conversion. The only thing we did was to instantiate a `dataFormat` instance with the `xmljson` type and configure its options for this specific transformation.

When the default options are good enough, there is no need to instantiate a data format instance. Instead, as part of the route, we only specify the operation type (`marshall`/`unmarshall`) and the data Format type:

```
<marshal><xmljson/></marshal>
```

There's more...

Message translator is a very general pattern and data transformations happen in many different places in Camel. We will see now different techniques for transforming messages and a very useful pattern for normalizing messages into a common format.

Type conversion

Type conversions happen very often in pipeline applications where a message is passed through multiple steps. Compared to data formats, these are simpler conversions, for example from `File` to `InputStream`, from `String` to `byte[]`, and so on. Camel handles these conversions transparently by maintaining an internal registry of available converters, and using them whenever needed. For example, whenever a message reaches a `Processor` that expects the payload to be from a different type, Camel will try to convert that message payload into the expected type using the type converters. If there are no type converters in the `TypeConverterRegistry` to convert the message from its current format to the expected format, then it will throw an exception and the processing will fail. Another occasion, when type conversion happens is when the message body is explicitly converted to a type as part of the routing:

```
from(...)
    .convertBodyTo(String.class)
    .to(...)
```

Or when the message body is requested in a specific type:

```
Document document = message.getBody(Document.class);
```

Transforming with expression language

The transform command followed by an expression is a quick and easy way to modify the message. Inside the transform command we can use any of the supported languages and access all fields of the `Exchange`: properties, headers, and in and out bodies. For example, using Simple language it is possible to do quick alterations to the message, or do full transformations using languages such as JQuery, XSLT, Groovy, Ruby, and so on.

```
</transform>
    <simple>New message ${body}</simple>
</transform>
```

Executing a Java method

When none of the existing solutions are good enough for the intended transformation, it is possible to do the job manually by executing a Java bean method. Depending on our needs, it is possible to annotate the method parameters and get different parts of the message, such as properties, headers, or body as method arguments:

```
.to("bean:myConverter?method=convert(${body}, ${header.userId})")
```

Instead of calling a custom bean, another option is to implement the `Processor` interface and call it as part of the route. The advantage of this approach is that we will get as the method parameter the actual `Exchange` object so we have full control over what transformation to do, and we can implement it inline as part of the route:

```
from("...")
    .process(new Processor() {
        public void process(Exchange exchange) throws Exception {
            exchange.getIn().setBody("Changed body");
        }
    })
    .to("...");
```

Using template component

There are Camel components which act literally as message translators. These are template components that convert the message into another format using a template file. Such components are XSLT, Velocity, FreeMarker, and Scalate.

Normalizing messages to a common format

In some occasions, semantically equivalent data is received in different formats from disparate sources and it has to be converted to a common data format for uniform processing throughout the system. In these situations using the **Normalizer** pattern can be a good way to go, as shown in the following diagram:

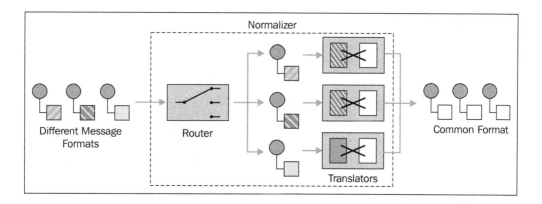

As we can see in the preceding diagram, the Normalizer uses a Context-Based Router to route each message to an appropriate message translator depending on the message format. Once the messages are transformed to a common format they all can be processed in a unified way. We can see example routes using this pattern in Spring XML or Java DSL at `http://camel.apache.org/normalizer.html`.

Splitting a message into many (Intermediate)

Messages passed to integration applications are not always in the right granularity to work with. In many cases they are composite messages consisting of multiple elements each of which has to be processed individually. This is when a **Splitter** pattern can help us to split incoming messages into series of messages, which are easier to work with. In this tutorial, we will create a route that splits an incoming XML message into multiple messages.

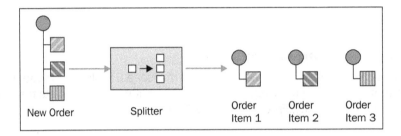

Getting ready

The complete source code for this tutorial is located under the project `camel-message-routing-examples/splitting-message`.

How to do it...

1. In the tutorial, we assume that the incoming message is an XML message in the following format:

```
<invoice>
    <item><product name="widget" quantity="2"/></item>
    <item><product name="gadget" quantity="1"/></item>
</invoice>
```

2. At the point in the Camel route where the message has to split into sub messages add the Splitter with the XPath expression:

```
from("direct:start")
    .split(xpath("//invoice/item/product"))
        .to("mock:products")
    .end()
    .to("mock:result");
```

How it works...

The only required configuration for Splitter is the criteria used to split the messages. It can be any expression language, so we have the freedom to choose from Simple language, XPath, XQuery, and many others, depending mainly on the message type and ease of splitting. In our example, to split the incoming XML we chose to use XPath expression that will be applied to the main message, and the sub messages will be sent to next endpoint(s).

There are a couple of options to customize the way newly created `Exchanges` are processed. With `onPrepareRef` it is possible to reference a `Processor` in the `Registry` that will be called just before sending the sub message to child endpoints. Setting `parallelProcessing` will cause new `Exchanges` to be processed in parallel instead of sequentially; `stopOnException` will interrupt further processing remaining sub messages if an Exception is thrown and return the error, whereas leaving the default `false` value will finish processing all sub messages and return the error at the end. Splitter also supports splitting messages using tokenizer expressions and splitting streamed messages, which is useful for chunking large files with a low memory footprint.

There's more...

In addition to splitting messages, the Splitter can also aggregate the messages back into one. This turns Splitter into a very powerful and compact construct used for splitting and then aggregating messages without a need for an additional Aggregator.

Aggregating results

When a message is passed to Splitter, it is split and the sub messages are sent to child endpoints, however, the processing is not over yet. If the incoming MEP is InOut, then Splitter has to reply to the caller or pass a message to the next processor in the route if there is one. This is where the `strategyRef` option comes into play. It allows us to reference a custom implementation of the `AggregationStrategy` interface from `Registry` used for aggregating results from the sub `Exchanges`. This interface only has one method that accepts the original incoming `Exchange` and the new `Exchange` returned from each sub `Exchange` that is processed:

```
Exchange aggregate(Exchange oldExchange, Exchange newExchange)
```

A typical implementation usually gets the result from `newExchange`, aggregates it into `oldExchange` and returns it. This allows accumulation of the sub `Exchange` results in the original `Exchange` and finally returning that as the final result from the Splitter. If no custom `AggregationStrategy` is used, the default strategy simply returns the original incoming `Exchange` without performing any aggregation.

`AggregationStrategy` is the same interface used in the Aggregator pattern (which we will see next), and having it as part of Splitter turns Splitter into a pattern having an embedded lightweight Aggregator.

Threading model

When `parallelProcessing` option is set, Splitter will create a new thread pool (`java.util.concurrent.ExecutorService`) and using this will process sub messages in parallel. Instead of creating a new thread pool, it is possible to share and reuse an existing thread pool by referencing it from the `Registry` using the `executorServiceRef` option.

Parallel processing with thread pools are also used in other EIPs such us Aggregator, multicast, WireTap, Recipient List, and some other components. Camel creates a new thread pool based on the thread pool profiles. The default thread pool profile looks like the following:

```
<threadPoolProfile id="defaultThreadPoolProfile"
    defaultProfile="true" poolSize="10" maxPoolSize="20"
      maxQueueSize="1000" rejectedPolicy="CallerRuns"/>
```

In the Java DSL, thread pool profiles are set using the `ExecutorServiceManager` field of `CamelContext`. If we use `executorServiceRef`, Camel will look up in `Registry` for a thread pool with the given ID. If there is no such thread pool, it will look up in `Registry` for a thread pool profile with the same ID. In case there is a thread pool profile with that ID, Camel will use it to create the new thread pool. If there is no such thread pool profile, default profile will be used. Also, all thread pools created by Camel will be properly shutdown when `CamelContext` is stopped, so we shouldn't worry about thread leaks. More details about the Camel threading model can be found on this page `http://camel.apache.org/threading-model.html`.

Aggregating multiple messages into one (Intermediate)

The Aggregator pattern is the opposite of the Splitter pattern; it combines multiple messages into one. In a message driven application, it usually appears after Splitter or the Recipient List patterns where a number of messages have been produced out of one, and the goal of the Aggregator is to merge back related messages. In this tutorial, we will create a route that merges messages belonging to the same group into one.

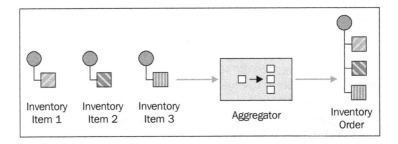

Inventory Item 1   Inventory Item 2   Inventory Item 3   Aggregator   Inventory Order

Getting ready

The complete source code for this tutorial is located under the project `camel-message-routing-examples/aggregating-messages`.

How to do it...

1. When using Aggregator, the first thing we have to decide is how the messages will be merged together. This is very specific to the actual message content and business logic of the application. We provide that logic by implementing the `AggregationStrategy` interface:

```
public class InvoiceTotalAggregator implements
  AggregationStrategy {
    public Exchange aggregate(Exchange oldExchange,
Exchange newExchange) {
        if (oldExchange == null) {
            return newExchange;
        }
        BigDecimal currentTotal =
oldExchange.getIn().getHeader("invoiceItemTotal",
  BigDecimal.class);
        BigDecimal itemTotal =
newExchange.getIn().getHeader("invoiceItemTotal",
  BigDecimal.class);
        oldExchange.getIn().setHeader("invoiceItemTotal",
currentTotal.add(itemTotal));
        return oldExchange;
    }
}
```

2. Then, we add the Aggregator to the route by referencing our custom aggregation strategy:

```
<bean id="invoiceTotalAggregator"
  class="org.apache.camel.howto.InvoiceTotalAggregator"/>

<camelContext
  xmlns="http://camel.apache.org/schema/spring">
    <route>
        <from uri="direct:start"/>
        <aggregate strategyRef="invoiceTotalAggregator"
completionTimeout="3000">
            <correlationExpression>
                <simple>header.invoiceId</simple>
            </correlationExpression>
```

```
            <to uri="mock:aggregated"/>
        </aggregate>
    </route>
</camelContext>
```

The Aggregator also has two other mandatory settings: the correlation expression and the completion condition. The first one is evaluated on each incoming message to generate a correlation key. The key is used to determine which messages should be grouped together. In our example, the key would be the `invoiceId`, so all invoice item messages belonging to the same invoice will be merged into one message. The completion condition is used to tell Camel when the aggregation is completed and the currently built message should be sent further down the route.

How it works...

When a new message comes in, the first thing done by the Aggregator is to evaluate the correlation expression and get the correlation key. Then the correlation key is used to look up the internal repository for an existing message with the same correlation key. The Aggregator has an internal (in memory by default) repository that contains the current aggregated `Exchange` for each correlation key. The next step is to pass the old `Exchange` (if there is one) and the new `Exchange` to the `AggregationStrategy` to merge them. After the aggregation, the completeness condition is checked, and if it is satisfied the aggregated `Exchange` is sent to the next processor in the route. If the aggregation has not completed yet, the internal repository is updated with the aggregated `Exchange`, and it continues waiting for the next `Exchange` to complete it or for timeout to occur.

There are a number of ways for specifying the completion condition and at least one should be present: `completionPredicate` is a `Predicate` expression which has to evaluate to true in order to complete the aggregated `Exchange`; `completionSize` states how many messages should be aggregated to complete the aggregation, it can be a fixed number or dynamically retrieved from the `Exchange` with an expression. `completionTimeout` is based on an inactivity period in milliseconds of the aggregated message, and completes the aggregated `Exchange` if there are no further incoming messages within the specified time period; `completionInterval` is similar but completes all currently aggregated messages after each time interval in milliseconds. The latter two completion conditions are asynchronous conditions, because these conditions are not evaluated on each incoming message, they run in a background thread and whenever a condition is satisfied the corresponding aggregated message starts its journey on the route.

There's more...

The Aggregator is usually used together with other patterns. Here are two common integration patterns that the Aggregator takes part in:

Composed message processor

This pattern is useful for maintaining the incoming message flow while processing each element of the composite messages in a separate flow.

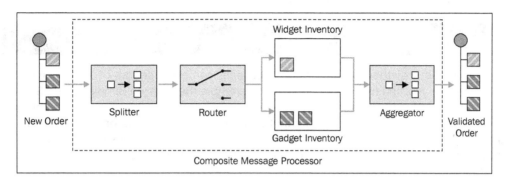

In the preceding routing diagram, we can see how the incoming composite message is split up into sub messages and then each sub message is routed to an appropriate destination using a Context-Based Router. After each sub message has been processed differently based on its type, they are aggregated back into a single message using Aggregator. Notice that the composed message processor pattern can also be achieved without using Aggregator explicitly. If you remember from the previous tutorial that Splitter has an embedded Aggregator in the form of `AggregationStrategy`. Using that strategy, Splitter can aggregate the results from each sub message and have the same effect as having an explicit Aggregator.

Scatter-gather

Here, a message is broadcast to multiple channels using the recipients list pattern or the publish subscribe mechanism. The difference in this case is that there is no Splitter involved, so each recipient gets the same copy of the incoming message.

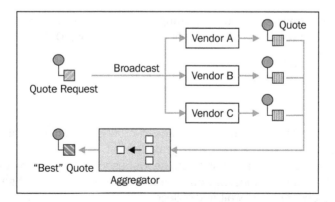

After the message has been processed by multiple recipients, Aggregator receives the results and produces one single result. In this scenario, Aggregator usually does not merge results; instead it picks up only one of them because they are identical, in the example in the preceding diagram – the **"Best" Quote**.

Reorganizing messages (Intermediate)

In an asynchronous distributed application, messages can easily get out of order. Sometimes, this is due to a limitation of some endpoints, for example the Amazon Simple Queue Service not guaranteeing in order delivery of messages. And sometimes, it is a conscious architectural decision (for example to increase throughput), maybe there is a Splitter or Context-Based Router used to split long running tasks into separate threads which is losing the original message order. No matter what the reason is, when the messages have to be (re)ordered, **Resequencer** is the pattern to use.

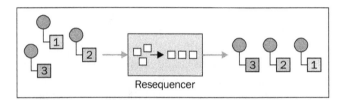

Resequencer

Getting ready

The complete source code for this tutorial is located under the project `camel-message-routing-examples/reorganizing-messages`.

How to do it...

Let's start with a route that is supposably getting random messages, and we want to put them back in order. Here is how a Resequencer definition looks in Java DSL:

```
from("direct:start")
    .resequence(header("message_index"))
    .batch().size(100).timeout(1000L)
    .to("mock:result");
```

The main piece of information Resequencer needs to know is the criteria that will be used to order the messages. This can be the message body itself, or a header or property and is specified using an expression. In addition to the header used for ordering messages, in our example there are two other options: `batchSize` and `batchTimeout`. These options control how long the Resequencer should wait and collect messages before sorting and letting them go.

How it works...

In the previous example, the Resequencer will collect up to 100 messages or will wait up to one second (whichever happens first), and then if there are any messages batched, sort them by the `message_index` header value, and let the messages further down the pipeline. When used in the default batching mode, Resequencer can also do reverse sorting, allow duplicate messages, and reject old messages or messages with an invalid sequence number. The downside of the batch processing algorithm is that it always collects messages up to a certain number or timeout, reducing the overall throughput of the system. There is also a stream based algorithm which reorders messages continuously based on detections of gaps between messages rather than fixed batch size. In order to use stream-based Resequencer, the messages must contain a unique sequence number for which the predecessor and successor is known. For example, the message sequence 1, 2, 4 has a gap, and the Resequencer will let message 1 and 2 go instantly without any batching, but retain message 4 until 3 arrives or timeout occurs. Configuring a streaming based Resequencer is very similar to a batch based one, except this one has the `timeout` and `capacity` options:

```
from("direct:start")
    .resequence(header("message_index"))
    .stream().capacity(100).timeout(1000L)
    .to("mock:result");
```

More information about the Resequencer pattern and how to use it can be found here at `http://camel.apache.org/resequencer.html`.

There's more...

There are two other patterns that work on the message flow without modifying the message content. Let's have a look at Throttler and Delayer patterns.

Limiting flow rate with Throttler

Throttler is a simple pattern useful for organizing messages in time. It works by throttling down messages to a specified maximum rate in order to protect a target endpoint from getting overloaded. For example, some APIs do not allow frequent calls or incur extra charges when a certain rate is exceeded. A snippet like the following will prevent the `mock:result` endpoint from getting more than three requests per 10 seconds during peak load times:

```
<route>
    <from uri="seda:a"/>
        <throttle maximumRequestsPerPeriod="3"
    timePeriodMillis="10000">
            <to uri="mock:result"/>
        </throttle>
</route>
```

The option `maximumRequestsPerPeriod` doesn't have to be hardcoded in the route definition, it can also be calculated at runtime using expressions.

Throttler can also work in non-blocking mode, so when the number of messages exceeds the maximum rate, instead of blocking the caller thread, it will schedule a task to be executed in the future using a separate thread. This lets the caller process further incoming messages while still honoring the maximum rate after the Throttler.

Delaying messages

The Delayer pattern functions very similar to Throttler, but instead of introducing delay only when the maximum rate is exceeded, it always delays the messages by the specified amount of time. One good use case for this pattern is route testing and simulating long running processes:

```
<route>
    <from uri="direct:start"/>
    <delay asyncDelayed="true">
        <constant>1000</constant>
    </delay>
    <to uri="mock:result"/>
</route>
```

Similarly for Throttler, it is possible to specify the delay option using expression or make it non-blocking using the `asyncDelayed` option.

Multicasting messages (Intermediate)

Multicasting is the process of delivering the same message to multiple recipients at the same time. When the list of recipients is specified dynamically it is known as a Recipient List pattern. Camel supports both static and dynamic recipients. In this tutorial, we will specify the recipients as part of the route definition, but the same options apply also for dynamic recipients.

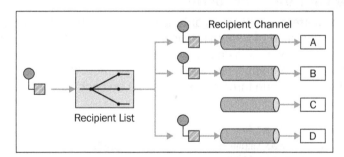

Getting ready

The complete source code for this tutorial is located under the project `camel-message-routing-examples/multicasting-messages`.

How to do it...

When using a static Recipient List, we hardcode the outbound channels as part of the route definition. We can also specify a custom `AggregationStrategy`, options for parallel processing, and whether to continue multicasting the message if an error occurs in any of the recipients.

```
from("direct:start")
    .multicast(new HighestQuoteAggregator())
        .parallelProcessing().stopOnException(false)
        .to("mock:a", "mock:b", "mock:c")
    .end()
    .to("mock:result");
```

How it works...

When a message reaches multicast, if the `parallelProcessing` options are not set, by default the message will be processed sequentially from the `mock:a`, `mock:b`, and `mock:c` endpoints. But, notice that this is different from processing a message sequentially in a pipeline style by a Camel route. The reason is that multicast will create a copy of the original `Exchange` for each recipient and `mock:b` will not see any changes done by `mock:a` or `mock:c`. Each of the recipients will get their own copy of the original incoming `Exchange`. One thing to keep in mind is that Camel will not do a deep copy and if we have any objects in the message body or headers, they will be shared across all recipients and potentially mutated concurrently. For these scenarios, a good place for making proper object copies is in the `onPrepareRef` Processor:

```
.onPrepareRef(new Processor() {
    @Override
    public void process(Exchange exchange) throws Exception {
        Order body = exchange.getIn().getBody(Order.class);
        Order clone = body.deepClone();
        exchange.getIn().setBody(clone);
    }
})
```

Similarly to Splitter and Aggregator, we can use a custom `AggregationStrategy` for aggregating replies from all recipients and create the outgoing message from the multicast. The default `AggregationStrategy` will simply pick up the last reply from the recipients.

Also, notice that we had to specify the end of the multicast definition, otherwise all the remaining endpoints from the route would also be considered as part of the multicast. Then, there are options which are common with the Splitter pattern: `executorServiceRef`, for custom thread pool, `stopOnException`, to stop broadcasting a message to the remaining recipients in case of errors, `shareUnitOfWork`, and so on. Sharing a unit of work allows multicasted `Exchanges` to report back any failures and propagate the exceptions to the original `Exchange`.

There's more...

There are two other Camel patterns which allow delivery of messages to multiple recipients: Recipient List which has very similar behavior to multicast but uses expression to choose the recipients dynamically; and Wire Tap which is a much simpler version of multicast and allows sending a copy of the incoming message to one additional recipient.

Dynamic multicasting

Using the Camel Recipient List is very similar to multicast, it supports the same options such as `strategyRef`, `parallelProcessing`, `stopOnException`, `onPrepareRef`, `shareUnitOfWork`, `streaming`, and `timeout`, which have the same effect. The main advantage of the `recipientList` statement is that it allows specifying the recipients dynamically using expression:

```
from("direct:a")
    .recipientList(header("recipients"));
```

A common way for specifying the recipients is with a header value as in the preceding example. The preceding example assumes that the `recipients` header is set by a previous step. The expression used in `recipientList` has to produce a result which is a `java.lang.Iterable` such as `java.util.Collection`, `java.util.Iterator`, array, `org.w3c.dom.NodeList`, or a comma separated string value. Any other result will be treated as a single value. The values in the collection have to be either endpoints or string which will be converted to `Endpoint` using URI syntax.

The Recipient List has two additional options: `delimiter` that let us change the default delimiter (which is comma) for string values; and `ignoreInvalidEndpoints` that tells whether to ignore unresolved endpoints or throw an exception.

Wire Tap

Wire Tap sends a copy of the incoming message to one separate channel while keeping the final destination of the message unchanged. By default, it will create a copy of the original message and process it using a separate thread pool in a fire-and-forget fashion.

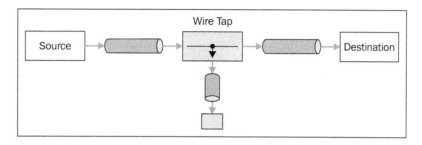

Wire Tap cannot deliver messages to more than one additional destination or use dynamic recipients. Also, it doesn't allow propagating exceptions by sharing a unit of work or stopping when an exception is encountered. It is mainly useful for monitoring, logging, and troubleshooting purposes. It is fully documented on this page `http://camel.apache.org/wire-tap.html`.

Error handling and monitoring (Advanced)

Integrating disparate applications through asynchronous messaging increases the possibility of failures, and makes error handling a mandatory part of every integration application. Camel offers a couple of mechanisms for handling and recovering from error conditions. In this tutorial, we will use **Dead Letter Channel** that retries failing requests and if the error remains, moves the failing message to a Dead Letter Queue (DLQ).

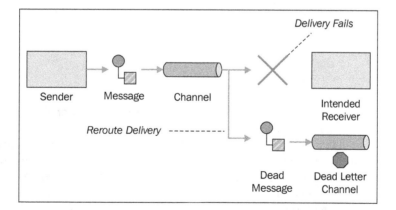

Getting ready

The complete source code for this tutorial is located under the project `camel-message-routing-examples/error-handling`.

How to do it...

An error handler can either be global, applying to all routes in a `CamelContext`, or applied to individual routes. There are different types of error handlers, each with different options and behaving slightly differently. In our example, we will create a `DeadLetterChannel` error handler applied to one route only.

1. We start with the `errorHandler` declaration, give it a `DeadLetterChannel` type, and configure its `redeliveryPolicy`:

```
<errorHandler id="deadLetterErrorHandler" type="DeadLetterChannel"
deadLetterUri="mock:error" useOriginalMessage="true">
    <redeliveryPolicy maximumRedeliveries="3"
redeliveryDelay="1000"
                        backOffMultiplier="2"
useExponentialBackOff="true"/>
</errorHandler>
```

2. Then, we apply the error handler to the route by its ID:

```
<route errorHandlerRef="deadLetterErrorHandler">
    <from uri="direct:start"/>
    <transform>
        <simple>${in.body} Modified data!</simple>
    </transform>
    <to uri="mock:result"/>
</route>
```

How it works...

As we already know, the consumer is responsible for receiving messages from other systems, creating an `Exchange` and then it starts routing it. If an error occurs before the routing of a message, for example, if the consumer cannot read a file from the file system, error handling will not be triggered. It is the responsibility of the consumer to deal with errors arising before the start of the routing process. Camel error handling applies only during routing of `Exchanges`. When a `Processor` (Endpoint or EIP) throws an exception during routing, Camel catches the exception and stores it in the `Exchange`'s `exception` field. The error handler kicks in only when the `Exchange` contains a caught exception. There are different error handlers available and one is always selected:

- **DefaultErrorHandler**: This is used by default if no other error handler is configured. It behaves similarly to a Java error handling mechanism. It doesn't perform any retries and propagates the exception back to the caller.

- **LoggingErrorHandler**: This logs the message along with the exception.

- **NoErrorHandler**: Camel always needs to have an error handler, using this dummy handler makes it behave as if there isn't any.

- **TransactionErrorHandler**: This is the default error handler used in transacted routes and requires a transaction manager to rollback the transactions for failed messages.

- **DeadLetterChannel**: This is the one used in our example. This error handler is an implementation of a Dead Letter Channel pattern where if a message cannot be delivered to its designated target, the message is moved to a different channel, which is quite often called a dead letter queue.

In our example, for the mandatory `deadLetterUri` option, we have specified `mock:error`, so if any error happens during the routing, the error handler will take the control, cleanup the exception from the `Exchange`, and move the message to this endpoint. Notice that `deadLetterUri` can also be another route with multiple steps, where we could still access the exception that caused the failure from an `Exchange` property:

```
Exception exception =
    exchange.getProperty(Exchange.EXCEPTION_CAUGHT,
      Exception.class);
```

The important thing to remember is that the exception field of the `Exchange` will be cleaned up and for the caller it looks like the `Exchange` has been processed successfully.

Usually in a route, we have multiple steps (processors), which are connected by channels, and each step can modify the message. When an exception is thrown from a processor, the channel responsible for that processor notices the exception and passes the control to the error handler. Depending on where the exception has occurred, it is possible that the `Exchange` has been modified from successfully completed processors and `DeadLetterChannel` will get a modified `Exchange`. To solve this problem, `errorHandler` has the `useOriginalMessage` option. When this option is set, `DeadLetterChannel` will receive an `Exchange` containing the original `In Message Body` that was passed to the route. So, in our example, if the `mock:result` throws an exception, even though the message body has been modified by the `transform` step, the `DeadLetterChannel`'s endpoint `mock:error` will receive the original message passed to the route. This option is useful for situations where we want to replay the failed `Exchanges` again to the same route using the original message.

Certain kinds of errors, for example caused by database deadlock, network failure, and so on are likely to succeed when retried a couple of times a little later. For these kinds of scenarios, `DeadLetterChannel`(and also `DefaultErrorHandler` and `TransactionErrorHandler`) offers a redelivery feature which is configured with a `RedeliveryPolicy`. For our example, we have allowed up to three retry attempts with a 1 second delay between the attempts. In addition, we have set it to exponentially back off and use `backOffMultiplier` of 2, so the second attempt will be done 2 seconds after the first one, and the third and final, attempt will be done 4 seconds after the second. If all of these attempts to process the request fail, only then the message will be moved to DLQ.

There's more...

There are two other mechanisms in Camel for dealing with erroneous situations: Exception Clause and `doTry-doCatch-doFinally` construct. The first one can be used together with error handlers, whereas the latter allows catching exceptions similarly to the Java language. Also, we will have quick look at monitoring and logging tools used with Camel.

Exception Clause

The Exception Clause allows us to specify error handling logic per exception type(s) in a route or the whole `CamelContext` scope. It is very flexible as we can have multiple Exception Clauses at any scope with one or multiple matching exceptions in each. Let's have a look at an example that has a route scope Exception Clauses applying for two Exception types:

```
<route>
    <from uri="direct:start"/>
    <onException>
        <exception>org.camel.ValidationException</exception>
        <exception>org.camel.OrderFailedException</exception>
        <redeliveryPolicy maximumRedeliveries="1"/>
        <handled>
            <constant>true</constant>
        </handled>
        <to uri="mock:error"/>
    </onException>
    <process ref="orderValidator"/>
    <to uri="mock:result"/>
</route>
```

When an error is thrown in a route, Camel will try to find the best matching Exception Clauses by going through all clauses from first to last (top-down) and then each declared exception type and comparing it to the thrown exception root cause. The comparison is done by starting from the root cause of the exception hierarchy, a top-down exception declaration compared to a bottom-up exception hierarchy. If an exact match is not found, Camel will try to find the closest matching exception using the `instanceof` operator. This comparison will match the Exception Clauses that has an exception type which is the closest superclass of the thrown Exception.

Once a matching Exception Clause is found, Camel will apply its `redeliveryPolicy` (if there is one) and other options such as `handled`, `continued`, and `useOriginalBody` before routing the message (if there are endpoints specified).

Java style error handling

Camel has the `doTry-doCatch-doFinally` construct for error handling which works in a similar way to Java's `try-catch-finally` blocks. It is not as flexible as error handlers or the Exception Clause but allows applying `try-catch-finally` logic in a route.

```
<route>
    <from uri="direct:start"/>
    <doTry>
        <process ref="orderValidator"/>
        <doCatch>
<exception>org.camel.ValidationException</exception>
<exception>org.camel.OrderFailedException</exception>
            <to uri="mock:catch"/>
        </doCatch>
        <doFinally>
            <to uri="mock:finally"/>
        </doFinally>
    </doTry>
</route>
```

Keep in mind that when `doTry-doCatch-doFinally` is used, the regular error handler and Exception Clause will not apply.

Monitoring and logging

In asynchronous message oriented applications, monitoring and logging play a more significant role. A graph of routes, where a message can move in any direction depending on rules evaluated at runtime, is not easy to troubleshoot. Luckily, Camel has various tools to help developers write messaging applications which are easy to monitor and debug. Here are a few of them:

▸ **JMX Support** (`http://camel.apache.org/camel-jmx.html`): Camel has extensive JMX support and allows monitoring and control of Camel managed objects through a JXM client. By default, the JMX instrumentation agent is enabled, and Camel will register the managed objects with `MbeanServer`. Supported managed types include `CamelContext`, `Routes`, `Endpoints`, `Components`, `Processors`, `ErrorHandlers`, and so on. We can connect to locally running `CamelContext` with a JMX client such as `JConsole`, see some performance statistics, and even interact with the objects. If the Camel process doesn't appear on the local connections list of the JMX client, we can connect to Camel by first running it with the RMI connector server enabled:

```
-Dorg.apache.camel.jmx.createRmiConnector=True
```

After enabling the RMI connector server connecting to it as a remote process using the following URL:

```
service:jmx:rmi:///jndi/rmi://localhost:1099/jmxrmi/camel
```

- ▸ **Hawtio**: This is a new hot management console for Java applications. It is a third party application with a plugin for Camel, and provides a web interface for visualizing and interacting with Camel routes. Worth trying it `http://hawt.io/`.

- ▸ **Log Component** (`http://camel.apache.org/log.html`): We have used logging in the examples so far to log each `Exchange`. But, log component can also run as a throughput logger where it aggregates statistics about `Exchanges` and logs them periodically or once a certain number of Exchanges are aggregated. The following endpoint will log stats for every 10 messages:

```
.to("log://org.apache.camel.howto?level=DEBUG&groupSize=10"
    )
```

Whereas, this one will log every 10 seconds only if there is at least one `Exchange`:

```
.to("log://org.apache.camel.howto?groupInterval=10000&group
    ActiveOnly=true")
```

Log component uses SL4J which supports Mapped Diagnostic Contexts (MDC). MDC is a technique used for stamping each log entry with contextual information for easier debugging and auditing complex distributed multithread applications. To get it working, we have to use a test kit that supports MDC (such as Log4j or logback) and enable it in Camel:

```
camelContext.setUseMDCLogging(true);
```

Then, in our log configuration (such as `lo4j.properties`), we can specify contextual information such as `exchangeId`, `messageId`, `routeId`, `camelContextId`, and so on:

```
log4j.appender.out.layout.ConversionPattern=%d [%-15.15t]
    %-5p %-30.30c{1} - %-10.10X{camel.exchangeId} - %-
    10.10X{camel.routeId} - %m%n
```

- ▸ **Tracer** (`http://camel.apache.org/tracer.html`): This is an `InterceptStrategy` which allows detailed tracing of routes. It logs how an `Exchange` moves from one endpoint to another during routing. By default, it is disabled, but we can enable it by running the Camel application with `-t` or trace arguments or by setting it programmatically to `CamelContext`:

```
camelContext.setTracing(true);
```

Testing the messaging applications (Advanced)

Integration applications are asynchronous, heterogeneous, and message driven in nature. Traditionally testing such applications is challenging, especially when there is not good tooling support. As a consequence, most of the testing is done manually at the end of the project with or without very little automated tests. Fortunately, Camel offers a variety of helper tools and makes writing routing tests a pleasurable activity. It can run routes isolated in a test container, mock external systems, specify expectations, trigger events, match expectations, simulate load or certain behavior, and so on. Let's see how to test a route written in Java DSL and then the additional tools and techniques used with Camel.

Getting ready

The complete source code for this tutorial is located under the following project: `camel-message-routing-examples/testing-routes`.

We will use `JUnit`, but there is also `TestNG` support, although it has fewer features.

```
<dependency>
    <groupId>junit</groupId>
    <artifactId>junit</artifactId>
    <version>${junit-version}</version>
    <scope>test</scope>
</dependency>
```

For testing applications using Java DSL we need the `camel-test` dependency:

```
<dependency>
    <groupId>org.apache.camel</groupId>
    <artifactId>camel-test</artifactId>
    <version>${camel-version}</version>
    <scope>test</scope>
</dependency>
```

How to do it...

1. Let's assume that we want to test the following route defined in Java DSL:

```java
public class SimpleChoiceRoute extends RouteBuilder {
@Override
public void configure() throws Exception {
    from("direct:start")
        .choice()
            .when(body().isEqualTo("orange"))
                .to("mock:oranges")
```

```
        .when(body().isEqualTo("apple"))
            .to("mock:apples");}
}
```

2. To test this route we have to extend the abstract `CamelTestSupport` class in our test and instantiate the route we want to test in the `createRouteBuilder` method:

```
public class SimpleChoiceRouteTest extends CamelTestSupport
    {
      @Override
      protected RouteBuilder createRouteBuilder() throws
    Exception {
            return new SimpleChoiceRoute();
      }
}
```

3. For each test, `CamelTestSupport` will create a `CamelContext`, run our route under test, and then tear everything down at the end of the test. Let's add our first test:

```
@Test
public void sendsAnAppleMessage() throws Exception {
    MockEndpoint mockOranges = getMockEndpoint("mock:oranges");
    MockEndpoint mockApples = getMockEndpoint("mock:apples");
    mockOranges.setExpectedMessageCount(0);
    mockApples.setExpectedMessageCount(1);

    template.sendBody("direct:start", "apple");
    mockOranges.assertIsSatisfied();
    mockApples.assertIsSatisfied();
}
```

4. The test method first gets hold of the mock endpoint and sets the expected number of messages, then using `producerTemplate` triggers an event and finally verifies that the expectation is matched. This is the general `expect-run-verify` test pattern. To make the test more readable, we could do a little bit of refactoring. For example, use annotations and declare `MockEndpoints` as instance variables, specify default `Endpoint` for `ProducerTemplate`, assert all mock endpoints in once step, and so on:

```
@Produce(uri = "direct:start")
protected ProducerTemplate start;

@EndpointInject(uri = "mock:oranges")
private MockEndpoint mockOranges;
```

```
@EndpointInject(uri = "mock:apples")
private MockEndpoint mockApples;

@Test
public void orderSomeFruits() throws Exception {
    mockOranges.expectedBodiesReceived("orange");
    mockApples.expectedBodiesReceived("apple");

    start.sendBody("orange");
    start.sendBody("apple");
    assertMockEndpointsSatisfied();
}
```

How it works...

CamelTestSupport is the base class for testing routes. During the setup stage, it will create a new CamelContext, producerTemplate, consumerTemplate, load the routes defined in the test class and start them. Then, in our test, we can access mock endpoints, set expectations and trigger events or directly send messages to the route endpoints using producerTemplate. At the end of each test method CamelTestSupport will stop the routes and CamelContext (unless it is configured to tear down everything at the end of all tests in the test class).

The base class also provides lots of other helpful methods and hooks to customize the test lifecycle. For example, in some cases it is required to set expectations or do some work before starting the routes. That is possible by overriding the isUseAdviceWith method to return true which will prevent CamelContext from starting automatically and it has to be started manually as part of tests:

```
@Override
public boolean isUseAdviceWith() {
    return true;
}
public void pollsFilesOnStart() throws Exception {
    getMockEndpoint("mock:result").expectedBodiesReceived("Some file
content");
    camelContext.start();
    assertMockEndpointsSatisfied();
}
```

Mock endpoint (`http://camel.apache.org/mock.html`) is another helpful tool used for testing routes. It is similar to other mocking libraries such as Mockito and jMock, and represents an inmemory list that collects all `Exchanges` it interacts with. It has mainly two types of methods: for specifying expectations and for verifying them, but it can also simulate specific behavior:

```
mockReplying.whenAnyExchangeReceived(new Processor() {
    @Override
    public void process(Exchange exchange) throws Exception {
        Message in = exchange.getIn();
        in.setBody("Mock response: " + in.getBody());
    }
});
```

The previous code snippet configures `mockReplying` to modify the message body when an `Exchange` is received in order to simulate the behavior of the mocked endpoint.

There's more...

Testing Spring XML DSL is no different, apart from using the Spring's `ApplicationContext` for creating the routes. Here, we will have a look at that and a few other testing tools.

Testing applications written in Spring XML DSL

To test Camel applications written in XML DSL, the camel-test-spring dependency is needed.

```
<dependency>
    <groupId>org.apache.camel</groupId>
    <artifactId>camel-test-spring</artifactId>
    <version>${camel-version}</version>
    <scope>test</scope>
</dependency>
```

The main difference to testing Java routes is that, instead of extending `CamelTestSupport`, the test class has to extend `CamelSpringTestSupport` and override `createApplicationContext`, rather than `createRouteBuilder`:

```
public class SimpleChoiceRouteSpringTest extends
  CamelSpringTestSupport {
    @Override
    protected AbstractApplicationContext
  createApplicationContext() {
        return new ClassPathXmlApplicationContext("META-
INF/spring/simple-choice-route-context.xml");
    }
    //the rest of the code is the same as previous
}
```

`CamelSpringTestSupport` provides feature-parity with `CamelTestSupport`, which means it allows tests to be written in the same style, provides the same protected variables, methods, and honors the same lifecycle. In fact we can use the same instance variables and test method from the previous example to test the Spring XML route.

There is also a way for running tests without extending the `CamelSpringTestSupport` class, called **Enhanced Spring Test Support**. In this scenario, the test class has to be annotated with `@RunWith(CamelSpringJUnit4ClassRunner.class)`, and use other annotation to inject Endpoints, CamelContext, and so on, because they are not available as protected fields of the parent class:

```
@RunWith(CamelSpringJUnit4ClassRunner.class)
@DirtiesContext(classMode =
  DirtiesContext.ClassMode.AFTER_EACH_TEST_METHOD)
@ContextConfiguration(locations = {"classpath:/META-
  INF/spring/simple-choice-route-context.xml"})
public class SimpleChoiceRouteEnhancedTest {
    @Autowired
    private CamelContext camelContext;

    @Produce(uri = "direct:start")
    protected ProducerTemplate start;
    //the rest of the class is the same as the example previous
}
```

The previous tests are mainly testing the message transformations and the routing logic in Camel routes. If the application interacts with external systems, there is also a need for integration testing to verify the interaction points. To see more testing techniques check the tests for the other examples from this book.

Other tools for testing

> ▸ **AdviceWith** (`http://camel.apache.org/advicewith.html`): Sometimes, a route has hardcoded Endpoints which makes it hard to test, or it might be necessary to modify part of the route before testing. For these kinds of scenarios Camel provides an Aspect-Oriented-Programing (AOP) model with the name `AdviceWith`. This feature makes it possible to modify the routes after they are loaded to `CamelContext` and provides methods to add, remove, and replace endpoints by name or ID.

> ▸ **NotifyBuilder** (`http://camel.apache.org/notifybuilder.html`): This allows testing routes without modifying them by building conditional expressions and then testing or waiting for that condition to occur. Good for integration testing with external endpoints.

> ▸ **DataSet** (`http://camel.apache.org/dataset.html`): The DataSet component provides a mechanism for easily performing load and soak testing of the system.

About Packt Publishing

Packt, pronounced 'packed', published its first book "*Mastering phpMyAdmin for Effective MySQL Management*" in April 2004 and subsequently continued to specialize in publishing highly focused books on specific technologies and solutions.

Our books and publications share the experiences of your fellow IT professionals in adapting and customizing today's systems, applications, and frameworks. Our solution based books give you the knowledge and power to customize the software and technologies you're using to get the job done. Packt books are more specific and less general than the IT books you have seen in the past. Our unique business model allows us to bring you more focused information, giving you more of what you need to know, and less of what you don't.

Packt is a modern, yet unique publishing company, which focuses on producing quality, cutting-edge books for communities of developers, administrators, and newbies alike. For more information, please visit our website: www.packtpub.com.

Writing for Packt

We welcome all inquiries from people who are interested in authoring. Book proposals should be sent to author@packtpub.com. If your book idea is still at an early stage and you would like to discuss it first before writing a formal book proposal, contact us; one of our commissioning editors will get in touch with you.

We're not just looking for published authors; if you have strong technical skills but no writing experience, our experienced editors can help you develop a writing career, or simply get some additional reward for your expertise.

Instant Apache ServiceMix How-to

ISBN: 978-1-84951-966-3   Paperback: 66 pages

Learn to create simple ServiceMix-based integration solutions using short, practical, hands-on recipes

1. Learn something new in an Instant! A short, fast, focused guide delivering immediate results.

2. Leverage OSGI to speed up the ESB deployment

3. Define message flow with Camel DSL

4. Expose your system via web services

Drools Developer's Cookbook

ISBN: 978-1-84951-196-4   Paperback: 310 pages

Over 40 recipes for creating a robust business rules implementation by using JBoss Drools rules

1. Master the newest Drools Expert, Fusion, Guvnor, Planner and jBPM5 features

2. Integrate Drools by using popular Java Frameworks

3. Part of Packt's Cookbook series: each recipe is independent and contains practical, step-by-step instructions to help you achieve your goal.

Please check **www.PacktPub.com** for information on our titles

Instant OSGi Starter

ISBN: 978-1-84951-992-2   Paperback: 58 pages

The essential guide to modular development with OSGi

1. Learn something new in an Instant! A short, fast, focused guide delivering immediate results.

2. Learn what can be done with OSGi and what it can bring to your development structure

3. Build your first application and deploy to an OSGi runtime that simplifies your experience

4. Discover an uncomplicated, conversational approach to learning OSGi for building and deploying modular applications

Web Services Testing with soapUI

ISBN: 978-1-84951-566-5   Paperback: 332 pages

Build high quality service-oriented solutions by learning easy and efficent web services testing with this practical, hands-on guide

1. Become more proficient in testing web services included in your service-oriented solutions

2. Find, analyze, reproduce bugs effectively by adhering to best web service testing approaches

3. Learn with clear step-by-step instructions and hands-on examples on various topics related to web services testing using soapUI

Please check **www.PacktPub.com** for information on our titles